Polka Dots!

by Sarah Tatler

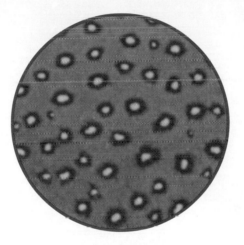

Celebration Press

An Imprint of Pearson Learning

I spot something with polka dots.

It's a strawberry. The dots on the strawberry are its seeds.

I spot something with polka dots.

It's a chameleon. The dots on the chameleon change color.

I spot something with polka dots.

It's a grouper. The dots on the grouper help it hide from other fish.

I spot something with polka dots.

It's a ladybug. The dots on the ladybug tell other bugs it tastes bad.

I spot something with polka dots.

It's a tiger lily. The dots on the tiger lily helped the flower get its name.

I spot something with polka dots.

It's a Dalmatian. The dots on the
Dalmatian are on its fur.

I spot something with polka dots.

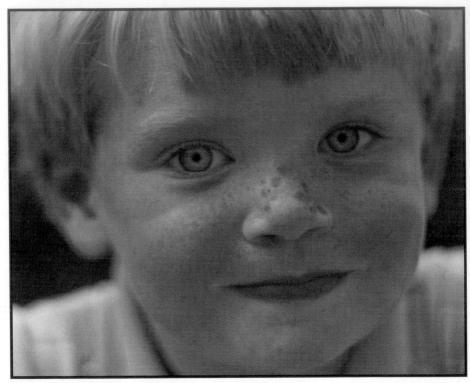

It's a kid! The dots on the kid are freckles. Can you spot something with polka dots?